# ANCIENT SCOTLAND

## Contents

# Stone Age People

## What was the Stone Age?

For thousands of years people in Scotland have seen these huge stones standing in the landscape. They mark a special place where people gathered long ago. They were put up at a time we call the Stone Age. People then did not know how to make things from metal. Many of their tools were made of stone.

Callanish, Isle of Lewis

# Hunters and fishermen

Scotland was once covered by ice hundreds of metres thick. Slowly, over 12,000 years ago, the climate became warmer and the ice melted. Ancient Scotland became a land of mountains, forests, rivers and lochs.

**This is how Scotland may have looked 9,000 years ago.**

Much of the low ground was marshy. Bears and wolves lived in the valleys which were thickly covered with shrubs and trees.

There were red deer and roe deer as well as wild cattle and wild boar. It was a good place for hunters and fishermen.

Early Stone Age visitors to Scotland came by boat about 9,000 years ago. This map shows some of the places they visited.

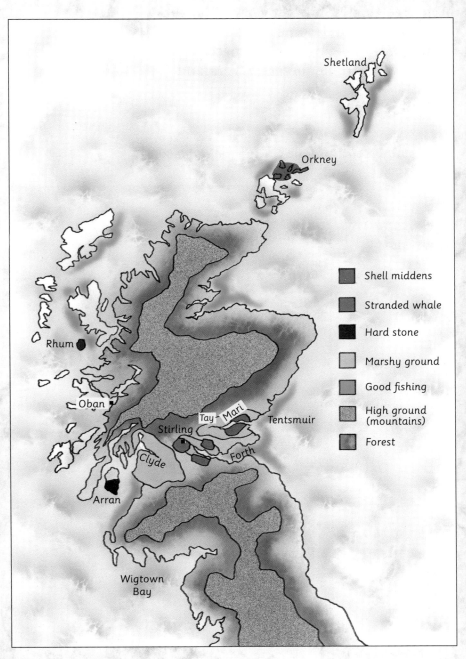

The spring and summer months were the best times for these visitors to paddle their skin covered canoes up the coast from the south of Britain. They looked for good harbours on the coast. Sometimes they went further inland by following the rivers.

Stone Age people made tools from bones and antlers as well as stone.

An ancient whale's skeleton was found near Stirling over a hundred years ago. There was a reindeer horn axe in its skull. How do you think this happened?

Early people would use the body of the whale for food. They used whale oil to provide light.

How would they use the whale bones?

**Why do you think boat was the best way to travel?**

The wandering Stone Age hunters also used a hard substance called flint to make tools and weapons. Flint was not easy to find. It could be chipped to make a very sharp cutting edge which was useful for scrapers, knives or the tips of spears and arrows. When flint is struck it can make sparks to light a fire.

These flint tools left by early hunters in Scotland were found in Fife.

*Flint tools from Morton Farm, Fife*

**How do you think they were used?**
**(Think about hunting and making clothes from animal skins.)**

This modern photograph shows someone trying to shape a flint tool.

**What other tool is he using?**

**Find:**

◆ **the pieces of flint which have been chipped away.**
◆ **the different stone hammers used to shape the flint.**

Stone Age people were nomads who moved from place to place. They stayed only as long as there was plenty of food to be found. As well as fishing and hunting they collected wild plants, berries and nuts. Then they moved on, but often they returned to the same places year after year.

**Archaeologists** have found some of the camp-sites of these early hunting bands. They can find out how people lived from the rubbish heaps they left behind. Some bone fish spears like these have been discovered.

**Stone Age people had no way to make fish hooks.**

**Find:**

◆ **the sharp points on the spears.**
◆ **the upward pointing notches cut into the bone.**

**How would they use these tools to catch fish?**

### Archaeologist

**Someone who finds out about the past from clues buried under the ground.**

Early people found lots of shellfish to eat along the shores of Scotland. Once they had eaten they threw the shells in a heap. When they went away at the end of the season, the shells were covered by sand. The next year more shells were added and the heap grew bigger as time passed.

On the island of Oronsay archaeologists have found huge mounds of shells and other remains left thousands of years ago by early hunters and fishermen. One mound is 30 metres across and 3.5 metres high.

These are finds from a camp in Fife used by early Stone Age people.

Finds from Morton Farm, Fife

**Oysters, mussels, limpets, winkles, cockles, whelks.**

## Farmers

A new group of people arrived in Scotland about 6,000 years ago. They still used stone tools and weapons. They still hunted for food but they knew how to farm as well. We call them New Stone Age people.

These new settlers looked for places along fertile rivers where they could grow crops of grain and keep their animals. Over a long time the weather had become warmer and drier. This made farming easier.

Because they were good farmers the New Stone Age people were able to store food. In the winter they had time to make finer stone tools. They smoothed and polished their tools and gave them a good cutting edge. They used heavy stone axes like these to cut down trees so that they could plant crops or hollow out logs for canoes.

**How do you think a handle was fixed to this axe?**

**What did the tool maker have to do to make smooth, polished axes like this?**

**How was the fine sharp edge made?**

The arrow heads which New Stone Age people made from flint were finely shaped so that they could be tied into the split ends of their wooden arrow shafts.

Where there was plenty of timber the New Stone Age farmers built wooden houses.

Looking at pictures taken from an aeroplane, archaeologists saw signs that there had been a building long ago beside the River Dee. New Stone Age people living about 5,600 years ago had built a long wooden house there.

How did the archaeologists know where to look? They looked from the air at crops growing in the fields below. When seeds are planted over the walls of an old building, they do not get as much moisture as the seeds in the rest of the field. The plants whose roots are above the wall will not grow so tall. The leaves may be less green. This shows up from the air.

An artist used the clues archaeologists found at Balbridie to make this drawing of how the long timber house may have looked.

**The house was nearly 25 metres long and 13 metres wide. There was nothing to see above ground because wood rots away. Only the holes dug to hold the posts for the house gave clues about its size.**

**Find:**
- **the wooden posts which form the walls.**
- **the thatched roof.**
- **the large posts marking the entrance.**

## Skara Brae

On Orkney, where there are few trees, it was easier to build
houses of stone. This is the inside of one. People began
living here about five thousand years ago.

All the furniture in this house is made of stone.

*Skara Brae, interior of House 7*

**Find:**

- ◆ the dresser.
- ◆ a stone bed which could be filled with heather.
- ◆ the hearth in the centre for the peat fire.
- ◆ tanks in the floor to keep shellfish for bait.
- ◆ stones for seats.
- ◆ the entrance to a cellar.
- ◆ cupboards in the wall.

To keep out strong winds and storms the people at Skara Brae built their houses inside their old rubbish heaps. There were passages between the houses so that you did not need to go outside to get from one house to another. This is the main passage.

**Find:**

◆ the huge flat stones used to roof the passage.
◆ the entrance to a house.
◆ the steps up to the doorway.
◆ the two large stones at the doorway.
One has fallen on its side.

People lived at Skara Brae for hundreds of years and farmed the land round about. We do not know exactly when or why Stone Age people stopped living there. Perhaps farming became difficult or a bad storm forced them to move. The empty houses were covered by a huge mound of sand. It was not until 1850 that a great storm swept away the top of the mound and the houses were seen once more.

**Which of these bone objects would be useful for:**

◆ jewellery?
◆ wearing in the hair?

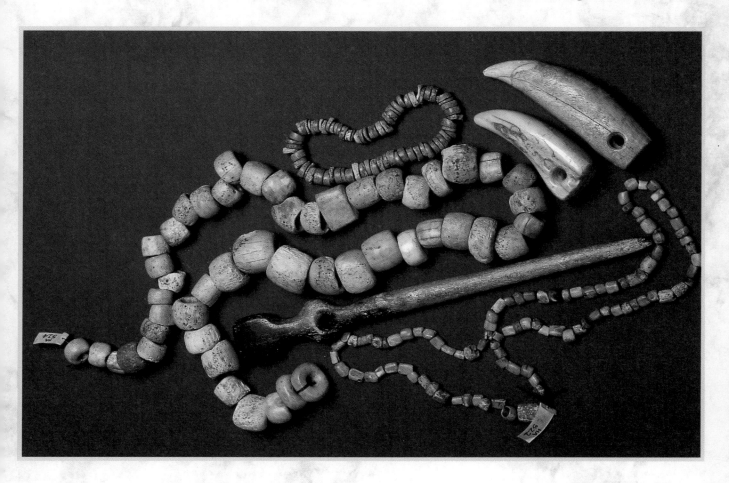

Traces of these things were found in the rubbish heap at Skara Brae:

• many bones of sheep and cattle.
• codfish bones.
• crab shells.
• other shellfish.
• bones of deer and pigs.
• egg shells.
• grains of barley.

These clues tell us a lot about what was eaten by the people who lived there.

Which food came from their farm animals?
Which food came from animals they hunted?
Which food did they grow in their fields?
Which food did they collect from the seashore or the countryside?

The people of Skara Brae made pottery. Clay hardens in the heat of a fire. The wet clay was shaped and decorated and then fired. This is a New Stone Age pottery bowl.

**Find:**

◆ **the scratched pattern.**

**How do you think it was made?**

Many of the things Stone Age people used have rotted away. They might have made wooden hoes or bowls or plates. Perhaps they had leather shoes or bags. Heather twigs would make baskets. They would need nets and snares. Since they left no spinning or weaving tools, it is likely that they wore clothes made from animal skins. We do not know.

## A Stone Age mystery

It took a very long time to shape and polish stone tools. They were very valuable to Stone Age people. Today you can see these carved stones in Montrose Museum. Stones of this kind have been found only in Scotland.

**Find:**

◆ a stone with a pattern of circles cut into it.
◆ a stone with many carved points.
◆ a stone with a number of round shapes.

Archaeologists wonder why early Stone Age farmers spent long hours carving stone balls which seem to have no use.

Some people think carved stones like these might have been:

- a magic weapon to throw.
- a good luck charm.
- for special ceremonies.
- connected with the sun or moon.

What do you think?

## Sacred places

Stone Age people in Scotland found many things they did not understand. Sometimes there were plenty of animals to hunt or fish to catch. At other times it was hard to find food. Farmers did their best, but some years their crops failed or their animals died. The moon appeared in the sky. The seasons changed from summer to winter. Storms or floods might cause great damage.

People wondered why these things happened. They tried to please the strange powers or gods who seemed to rule their lives.

New Stone Age people believed that the way they were buried was very important. When chief people died, they were placed in great burial **cairns**. There are over a thousand cairns in Scotland. This one is not far from Skara Brae.

Maeshowe, Orkney

**Find:**

◆ **the ditch round the cairn.**

A great number of people were needed to build such a large **tomb**. The work must have taken a very long time.

---

**Cairn**

**A mound of stones above a place where someone was buried in earlier times.**

---

**Tomb**

**A place specially made for burying dead bodies.**

Inside this huge cairn, which is 32 metres long and 13 metres wide, archaeologists found this room and the bones of twenty six people. The bones show that the people were not tall and did not live long. They had rheumatism and probably died by the time they were twenty five.

Midhowe Cairn, Orkney

**Find:**

◆ **the large slabs of stone which divide each side into sections.**

**They are so well fitted and smoothed that it is very hard to push a knife between the stones.**

**Bones of animals and birds found outside at the door show that special feasts were held there.**

New Stone Age people built special places where they could carry out ceremonies to please their gods, like this circle of giant stones. Sometimes they made a ditch all round.

*Ring of Brogar, Orkney*

Later people who moved into Scotland still used these sacred places and sometimes added to them.

We do not know how people used these circles. Archaeologists think they show that people were interested in the rising and setting of the sun and the moon.

A great many people must have worked hard to move and set up the stones. Some stones were dragged for miles over rough ground on rollers or sledges. There were no carts.

Very deep holes had to be dug out with stone tools. The builders worked together to haul and push the stones to make them stand up. Finally the stones were wedged with earth or stones. The builders did such a good job that 5,000 years later many of the stone circles are still standing.

Loanhead of Daviot, Aberdeenshire

Huge flat stones like this one in Aberdeenshire weigh up to 61 tonnes. Stone Age people managed to move it 10 km to the circle.

**Find:**

◆ **the two large stones standing at the side.**

**Archaeologists think they are arranged with the huge stone in the centre to frame the moon when it is looked at from inside the circle.**

# Bronze Age People

## What was the Bronze Age?

New settlers crossed the North Sea about 4,000 years ago. Others came to Scotland from Ireland. Some of the settlers had an important secret. They knew how to use **bronze** to make tools and weapons instead of using stone. They also used it to make jewellery and useful things like this bucket. We call this time the Bronze Age.

From Flanders Moss, Perthshire

**Find:**

◆ the two handles.

**How might they be used if the bucket was very heavy to carry?**

**How might the bucket be used to cook things over a fire?**

| Bronze |
| --- |
| A metal made by mixing copper and tin. |

# Beaker people

Not everyone began to use bronze tools right away. For a
long time there were places where people still used only
stone tools. Things changed slowly.

From Edzall, Angus

The new settlers found good places to land at the mouths of
the River Dee and the River Don where Aberdeen now
stands. These people were farmers too. They cut clearings
in the forests to grow barley. They kept sheep, goats, pigs
and cattle. As well as using metal, these settlers made a
special kind of pottery with a wide opening at the top.
Because of this beaker shaped pottery, archaeologists call
them the Beaker People.

**Find:**

◆ **the different lines which have been scratched into the wet
clay to decorate this beaker.**

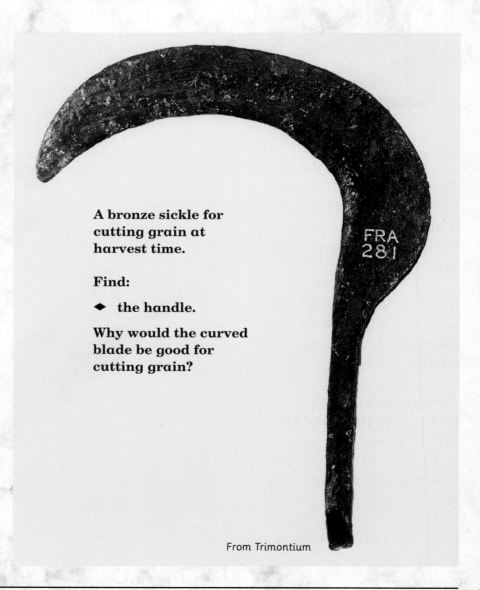

**A bronze sickle for
cutting grain at
harvest time.**

**Find:**

◆ **the handle.**

**Why would the curved
blade be good for
cutting grain?**

From Trimontium

Bronze metal tools such as
sickles and axes made
farm work easier.

Farmers had always grown
crops on the hillsides
because of the thick
undergrowth of trees and
shrubs in the glens. Now
they were able to clear
fields in these valley
bottoms. They did not have
to move away in search of
food. They began to live in
larger groups which grew
into large tribes.

## Metal workers and traders

The smiths who were able to make things out of metal were very important people. Because they were skilled at working copper, bronze or gold, they did not have to do farming work as others did.

They knew how to shape the metal to make tools and weapons with sharp cutting edges and finely decorated ornaments and jewellery.

The smiths cut the shape of an axe in soft stone in two halves to make a mould like this.

**Find:**
- the shape cut in the stone.
- the marks made in the stone to match up the two sides of the mould.

*From Sittenham*

The two sides of the mould were bound together so that the hollow on the inside was the shape of an axe.

A small clay pot was used to melt the bronze over a fire ready to pour into the mould.

They poured the molten bronze into the stone block and let it cool.

The stone mould was removed.

Here is a bronze axe ready to use.

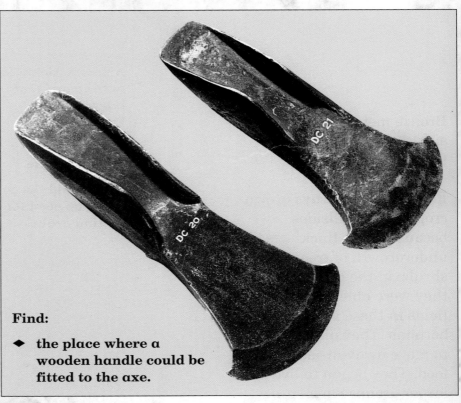

**Find:**
- the place where a wooden handle could be fitted to the axe.

*Found near Peebles*

The Bronze Age in Scotland lasted well over one thousand five hundred years. The climate slowly changed again, becoming colder and wetter. It was not so easy to farm well. People had to fight to keep their good land and crops and protect their homes. As the number of people grew bigger, they banded together under new leaders and built hill-top forts to defend themselves.

*The White Caterthun*

**Find:**

◆ **the round shape of the hill-fort seen from the air.**

◆ **the rings of defences round the fort.**

People who were afraid of attack sometimes buried all the valuable things they thought enemies might steal.

Beautiful Bronze Age swords, daggers and shields have been found. Many weapons like these were made over 2,500 years ago.

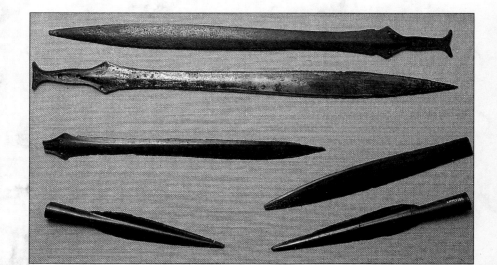

**You can see these bronze swords today in the Montrose Museum.**

**No one came back to dig up these buried treasures. What might have happened to the owners?**

People were eager to have the tools, weapons or jewellery made by the Bronze Age smiths. Instead of hunting or farming the smiths spent their time making things which they could exchange for food or clothes.

Bronze tools were more useful than stone tools. If they grew blunt they could be hammered sharp again. If they broke, the metal could be melted down to make new tools. Richer, more powerful farmers and warriors wanted special ornaments and jewellery to show how important they were.

The smiths were specialists. That meant they spent all their time working at one particular job. Some made tools. Some made weapons. Others made ornaments or jewellery like these bronze necklaces and bracelets.

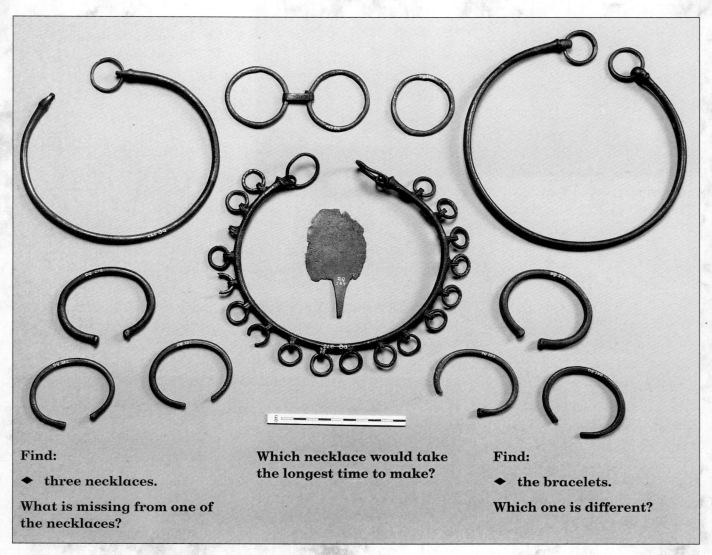

**Find:**

◆  three necklaces.

**What is missing from one of the necklaces?**

**Which necklace would take the longest time to make?**

**Find:**

◆  the bracelets.

**Which one is different?**

*From Braes of Gight, Aberdeenshire*

Sometimes copper was found on the surface of rocks in some parts of Ancient Scotland. People knew where to find gold in the hills or washed down in the fast flowing streams. Gold and copper are soft metals and can be easily beaten into shape.

But smiths needed tin to mix with copper to make bronze. There was no tin in Scotland.

The smiths had to **import** tin from far away places. Find them on the map.

| **Import** |
| --- |
| **To bring in goods from another country.** |

| **Export** |
| --- |
| **To send goods to another country.** |

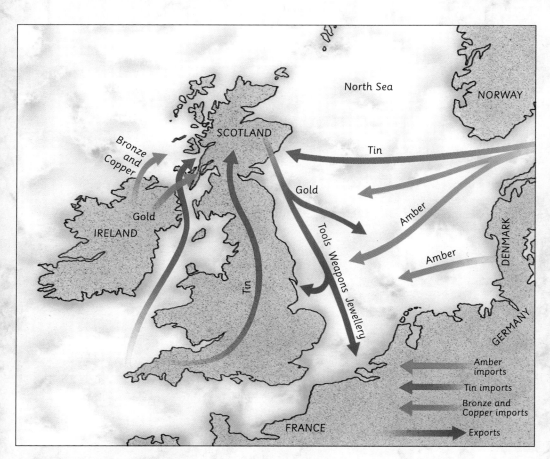

Sometimes the traders brought beautiful gold, copper or beaten bronze goods from the continent of Europe. Sometimes they had jewellery made of amber. In every village where they stopped, people would rush to see what they had brought. There was no money. If people wanted anything from the traders they had to offer something the traders wanted in return.

**This map shows trade in the Bronze Age.**

**Find:**

- the places where amber could be found.
- what metals came from Ireland to Scotland.

**Since tin was so important, the smiths would have to give something valuable in exchange. What might they give the traders who brought the tin?**

| **Traders** |
| --- |
| **People who take the goods they have to another place and exchange them for something different.** |

| **Amber** |
| --- |
| **A special kind of sap which comes from some trees. When it is hard it can be carved and polished.** |

## Burying the dead

Like the New Stone Age people, the new settlers of the Bronze Age believed that the way people were buried was very important.

Sometimes a dead person was buried in a grave like this called a **kist**. It was made of stone slabs. There was a stone slab on the top of the kist.

Montrose Museum

The dead body was laid on its side in a crouching position. How do you think archaeologists work this out?

### Kist

**A box shaped burial chamber made from stone slabs.**

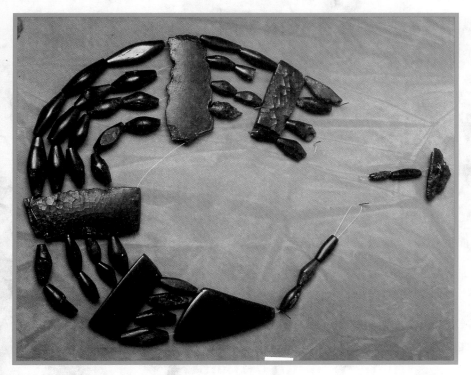

From Melgund, Angus

When a farmer in Angus was ploughing his field, he found a kist. He told archaeologists. Inside they found this jet necklace with the body.

**What part of the necklace is missing?**

**Why do you think the necklace was buried?**

Although people often still used the same sacred places as in earlier times, they also began to put the ashes of the dead into pottery urns like this one.

**Find the pattern on the urn. How do you think it was made?**

From Aberlemno, Angus

# The Celts

## Who were the Celts?

The Bronze Age farmers traded with a people called Celts who crossed into Britain about 2,500 years ago. The Celts spoke a language similar to the Gaelic spoken in parts of Scotland today.

They knew how to use iron ore to make strong weapons of iron, a much harder metal than bronze. Their iron swords and spears helped them to conquer the local people. Their iron ploughshares helped them to plough more deeply. They could farm land the Bronze Age farmers found difficult.

We call this time the Iron Age.

The Celts were such skilful workers in metal that they made beautiful jewellery like this end piece of a necklace.

From Cairnmuir, Peebleshire

# An Iron Age house

The Celts who settled in Scotland used iron axes to cut down trees and lived much like the Bronze Age farmers. Round their villages they built strong wooden fences or stone walls to keep out warlike neighbours. The houses inside were round with thatched roofs.

At Green Knowe in Peebleshire archaeologists have been able to work out how an Iron Age house was built. An artist made this drawing from the clues they found.

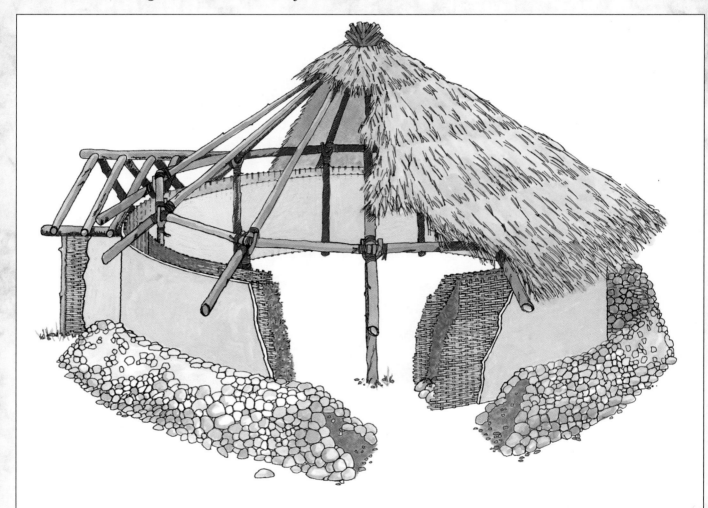

Find:

◆ the entrance. It was like a porch with a sloping roof.
◆ the wall round the house. Why is it there?
◆ the two woven screens made of branches plastered with clay. The heather packed inside helped to keep the house warm.
◆ the low wall in between the screens. How would this strengthen the house?
◆ the posts which hold up the roof. How are they joined to the roof timbers?
◆ the pointed roof covered with thatch.

# Home life

The inside of the Iron Age house probably looked like this.

**Everybody had jobs to do.**

Find:

- the fire in the middle of the floor. They boiled meat in a large pot hung over the fire. Sometimes they used a cooking pit. To heat the water in it they dropped in red hot stones.

Why would the sparks from the fire be a danger?

- the girl grinding grain to make flour for bread. This took a long time.
- the clay oven near the fire where the bread was baked.
- the meat hanging in the rafters. The smoke helped to keep the meat from going bad.
- the woman weaving. Iron Age people spun thread and wove cloth for their clothes and rugs.
- the bed made from a pile of straw with a rug on top.

The Celts liked bright clothes with striped or checked patterns on them. Women wore long dresses. Men wore tunics and trousers with woollen cloaks. The women wove woollen material for their families like this piece of cloth found at Falkirk.

**Find:**

◆ the checked pattern.

**This is the earliest known piece of tartan cloth in Scotland. The cloth was coloured with dyes made from plants.**

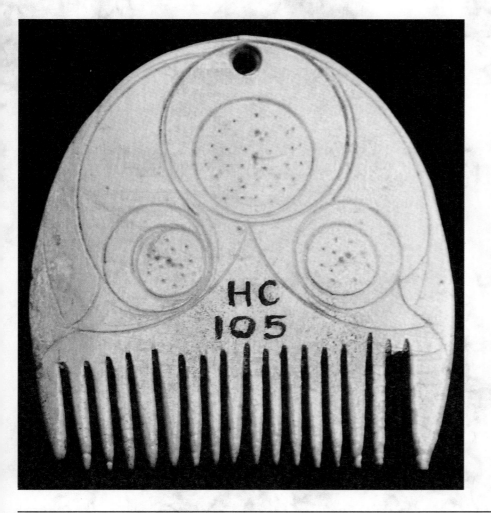

The Celts liked to dress up.

Archaeologists think the women used herbs and berries to redden their cheeks and lips and paint their fingernails. They wore their hair long and used combs like this as ornaments.

**The Celts were fine artists who loved to decorate the objects they made with beautiful patterns.**

**Find:**

◆ the decorated pattern on the comb.

**How has the comb been damaged?**

## Celtic warriors

By 2,000 years ago there were sixteen
large tribes of Celts in Scotland. They
often fought each other, stole cattle and
attacked villages. Warriors were very
important to the tribe. They were proud to
be able to fight well in battle but they did
not spend all their time fighting. The Celts
were also very good artists and craftsmen
who made fine tools, weapons, clothes and
ornaments.

Celtic warriors fought with long slashing
swords and spears made of iron.

The craftsman who made this bronze
sword holder, called a scabbard, skilfully
used two different shades of bronze.

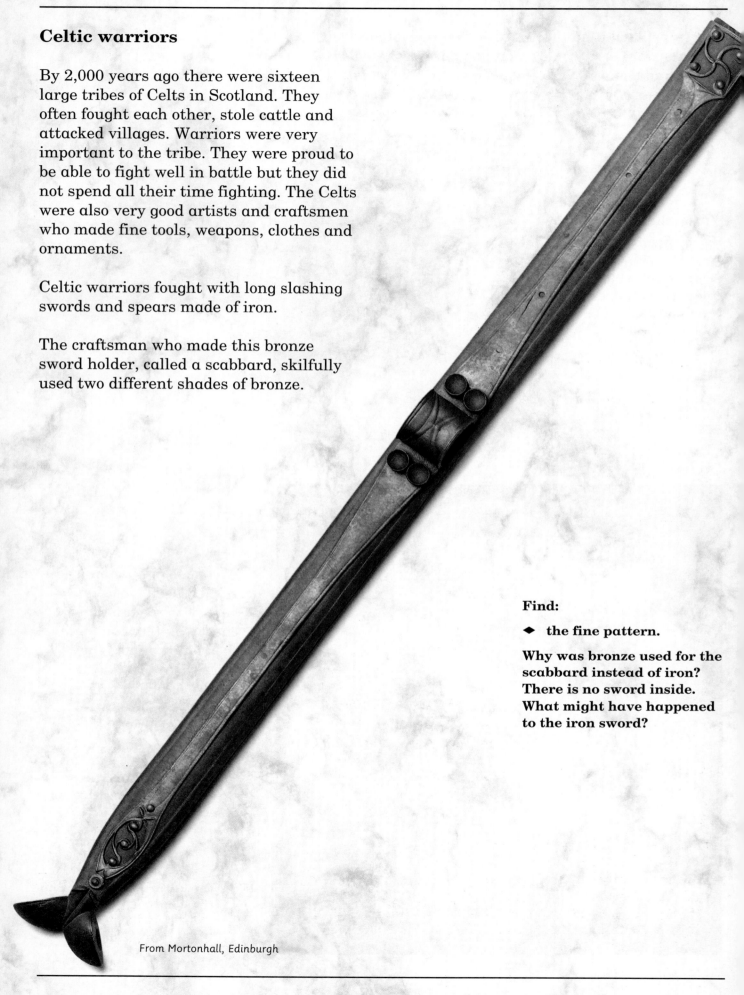

From Mortonhall, Edinburgh

**Find:**

◆ the fine pattern.

Why was bronze used for the
scabbard instead of iron?
There is no sword inside.
What might have happened
to the iron sword?

The Celts tried to frighten their enemies even before a battle began. They made themselves look very fierce. Sometimes they wore leather helmets but often they used **lime** to make their long hair stick out from their heads. They wore cloaks, trousers and tunics dyed in bright colours. Some warriors believed it was braver to fight with no clothes on. They wore only a splendid gold torc like this round their necks.

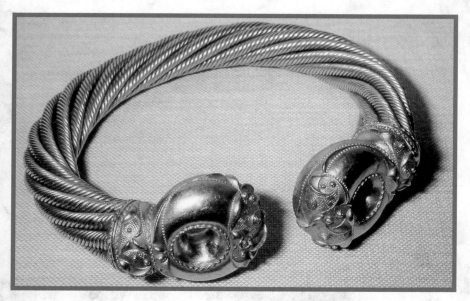

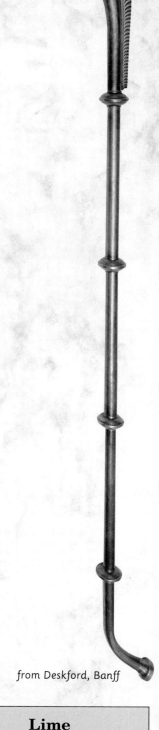

**Find:**

◆ the beautifully decorated ends of the torc which would be worn at the front.

The rest of the torc is made from eight fine strands of gold twisted into one thicker strand. Often craftsmen used gold collected from the streams that flowed into the River Clyde.

When the Celts fought in battle the most frightening thing was the terrifying noise. The warriors gave fierce battle cries as they charged. Their long bronze war trumpets were carved with the head of a boar, like this one found nearly two hundred years ago in Banff.

**The craftsman who made the trumpet tried to make it as frightening as possible.**

**Find:**

◆ the boar's head. The Celts thought the wild boar was a brave animal which never ran from its enemies.
◆ the eyes which would be painted red, the colour of battle.
◆ the mouth which had a moving tongue inside. When the trumpet sounded it made a noise like a screaming pig.
◆ the long tube as tall as a man which scientists believe was attached to the boar's head.

*from Deskford, Banff*

---

**Lime**

**A white powder made by heating limestone.**

---

This panel from Denmark shows Celtic warriors ready for battle.

*The Gundestrop Cauldron*

**Find:**

- the foot soldiers. They have swords, spears with huge iron blades and long shields made of leather.
- the trumpets with moving tongues. How many can you see? How are they played?

Some soldiers went into battle on horseback. When they were fighting in the open the chief Celts often used fast two-wheeled chariots like the one in this modern picture.

**Find:**

- the iron-rimmed wheels of the chariot.
- the open back of the chariot which allowed the warrior to leap down quickly. His job was to slice off as many enemy heads as possible.

- The skilful charioteer who drove the ponies at full gallop against the enemy. He had to get the warrior into the best position to fight and be ready to move in and pick up the warrior when needed.

## Gods and goddesses

The Celts believed in many gods and goddesses. Each tribe had its own special father god and mother earth goddess who helped them in battle and made the crops grow well. The people gave offerings called sacrifices to gods like this one when they hoped for a good harvest.

*A Celtic fertility god from Blackness Castle*

Sometimes an animal was sacrificed and sometimes perhaps people!

The Celts believed that spirits lived in wells and streams, near burial grounds, on hill tops or among the trees. They thought that people went to the Otherworld when they died so they put things in the grave which they thought they might need.

Magic was important to the Celts. Today we still do some of the things which the Celts believed brought good luck. They sometimes threw gold or other valuable things into water to please the god who stayed there. Some people today throw coins into a well because they think it is lucky.

At certain times of the year the Celts held special feasts and celebrations as we do nowadays. The feast at the start of winter was held at the time we have Hallowe'en.

## Strong places

Life in the Iron Age was often dangerous. Tribes sometimes attacked each other. People tried to build strong places where they would be safe. One way was to build forts on high ground with a good view of the countryside around like the two hillforts in this picture.

**Find:**

◆ the two forts. What shape are they?

◆ the thick walls of earth and stone in rings round each hill. How would they make it hard for an enemy to attack the fort? Sometimes timber was built into the walls to strengthen them.

◆ the space in the middle where people would stay in the fort. Many people only lived in the fort when an enemy attacked.

◆ the land at the foot of the hill where people could grow crops and keep animals.

*The Caterthuns, Angus*

Some tribes built forts on hills known as **duns**. One famous fort was Duneiden which is now Edinburgh. Do you know any places in Scotland whose name begins with dun (e.g. Dunfermline)?

There are the remains of more than fifteen hundred hill forts in Scotland. Some forts were quite small where only a few families lived. Others such as the hill fort at Eildon Hill near Melrose were very important places, like a small town, where a great chieftain lived.

| **Dun** |
| --- |
| **A strong hill fort built by Celts.** |

Farmers living in low-lying marshy country tried to make their homes safe from attack by building them in the water.

Sometimes they used an island in the middle of a loch. Sometimes they made small artificial islands close to the loch shore where it was marshy. They piled up layers of logs and branches, stones and clay. Then they pushed strong wooden piles through the layers to make islands, called 'crannogs', like this one on Loch Awe.

Loch Awe, Argyll

**Some crannogs have disappeared under the water. Along the shores of Loch Awe divers have found twenty crannogs.**

**Find:**

◆ **the artificial island.**

**Why do you think it was built close to the shore?**

**Why is it difficult to spot a crannog nowadays unless a diver looks for it?**

The crannog dwellers had to paddle to dry land in their canoes. Some built a narrow road to the shore just below the surface of the loch. They could keep their animals and grow their crops in the fields. If danger threatened they could hurry back to the crannog.

About 2,000 years ago the peoples of Ancient Scotland began to build strong stone towers called brochs with huge walls 15 to 20 metres high. Although there are over five hundred of them in Scotland, no one really knows why they were built. This broch in Shetland is built close to the shore.

**Find:**

◆ the broch.

**Why would the builders make it wider at the base?**

**Would it be a good place to shelter from enemies?**

*Broch of Mousa, Shetland*

Some people think the brochs were built to guard against a new invader – the Romans.

This is how a broch may have looked in Celtic times.

**Find:**

◆ the wall round the broch. Why is it there? What other buildings can you see inside?
◆ the gate in the wall. How do people enter the broch? Why has the doorway been made small and difficult to get at? In some brochs the only way in was a low, narrow tunnel.
◆ the open top of the broch which lets in light and air. Why are there no windows?
◆ the thatched roof which partly covers the double wall of the broch. There was a hollow space underneath with a stone staircase and galleries inside. How would these be used?
◆ the people in the picture. What are they doing? How might things change if an enemy appeared?

**Do you think the brochs would be comfortable to live in for long?**

## Earth houses

In some places in Scotland archaeologists
have found strange underground buildings
which they call 'earth houses'. They were
not really houses. No one lived in them
although small houses have been found
close by above ground.

Ardestie, Angus

**Find:**

◆ the long passage lined with stone,
perhaps used to store things.
◆ the drain running down the centre of the
passage.
◆ the remains of other buildings on the left.
What shape are they? How might they
have been used?

The earth houses were cool and dry. Some people think they
might have stored grain or other food for more than one
family. Others have suggested that animals were kept in
them. No one knows for certain.

# Romans and Caledonians

## The Romans invade

The Roman emperor Hadrian ordered this wall to be built about 1,900 years ago. He wanted to protect Roman Britain from attack by the Celtic people of the north.

The wall of stone is 117 kilometres long and 6.5 metres high.

**Find:**

◆ the wall stretching out across the country.

**Why is it not built in a straight line?**

**What would be needed to build the wall?**

The Romans were very good at fighting. Over two thousand years ago their powerful armies took over all the other towns and people in Italy. Then they conquered the lands of other people in Europe so that they ruled a large empire. Find it on the map.

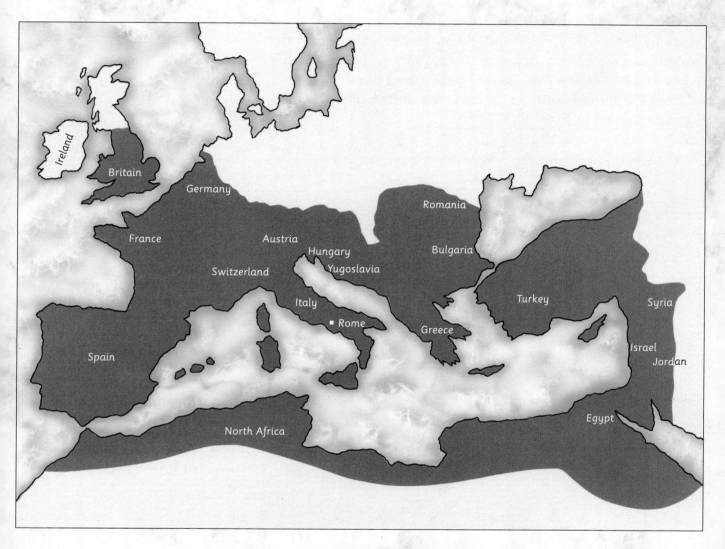

**Which part of Britain was not part of the Roman Empire?**

Twice the Roman army invaded Britain. After many battles the Romans were able to beat the Celts in the south. The Romans built roads and towns and used their large, well-trained armies to keep control. The Celts in the south of Britain followed the Roman rule and way of life for nearly four hundred years.

Things were very different in the north. Scotland was the wild north-west **frontier** of the Roman Empire. The Romans called the people there Caledonians.

**Frontier**

The border between one place and another.

# Roman forts

The Romans wanted to control the whole of Britain. In AD 78, thirty five years after the Romans invaded the south of Britain, the Roman general Agricola came north with a large army. The Celts in Scotland were not so well organised. They found it hard to stop Agricola's army. Some tribes in the south of Scotland made friends with him. They traded food for Roman ornaments, pottery and glass. Other tribes fought. As the Roman army marched north the soldiers built roads and forts. The map shows how the Romans moved in Scotland.

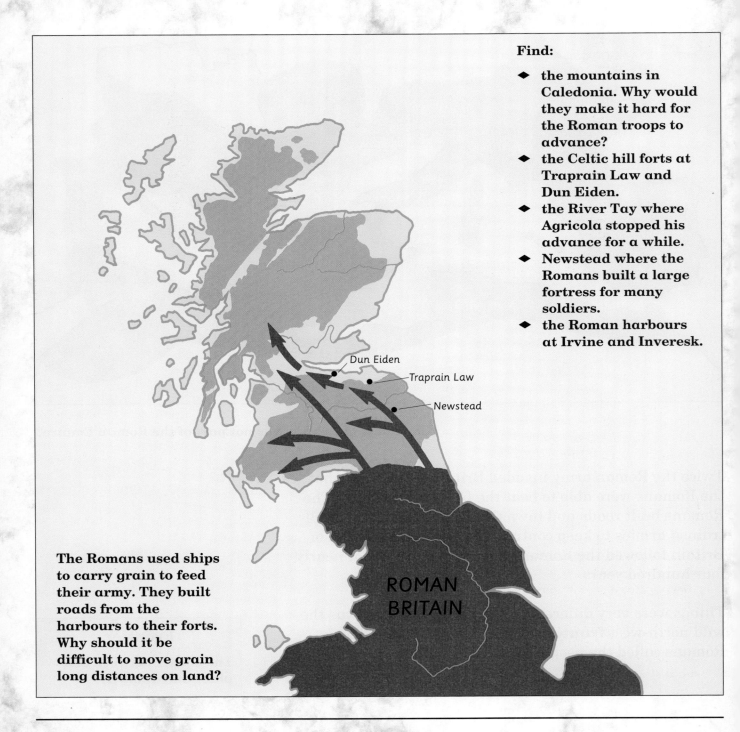

**Find:**

◆ the mountains in Caledonia. Why would they make it hard for the Roman troops to advance?

◆ the Celtic hill forts at Traprain Law and Dun Eiden.

◆ the River Tay where Agricola stopped his advance for a while.

◆ Newstead where the Romans built a large fortress for many soldiers.

◆ the Roman harbours at Irvine and Inveresk.

Dun Eiden

Traprain Law

Newstead

ROMAN BRITAIN

**The Romans used ships to carry grain to feed their army. They built roads from the harbours to their forts. Why should it be difficult to move grain long distances on land?**

As well as large forts for about five hundred men the Romans built smaller forts as they advanced. The plan shows the fort at Cadder.

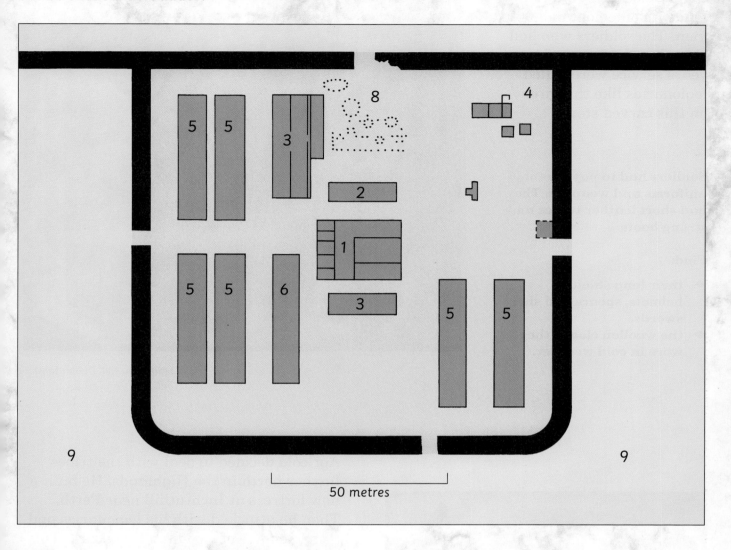

50 metres

**Find:**

- the gates.
- the road leading from the gate to the headquarters.
- the main road joining the two side gates which passes in front of the headquarters.
- the soldiers' barracks.
- the wall round the fort.
- the ditches in front of the wall. How would they make it hard to attack the fort?
- the grain stores and supply stores. Why were they important?
- the bath house. What would the pits be for?

| Key | |
|---|---|
| 1 | Headquarters |
| 2–3 | Stores for grain |
| 4 | Bath house |
| 5 | Barracks for soldiers |
| 6 | Storehouse |
| 7 | Workshops |
| 8 | Pits |
| 9 | Ditches |

## Roman soldiers

The Roman army was made up of legions of 5,000 men. The soldiers who had signed on for twenty five years service were called legionaries like the three on this carved stone.

**Soldiers had to pay for their uniforms and weapons. They had short leather tunics and strong boots.**

**Find:**

- **their long shields, helmets, spears and short swords.**
- **the woollen cloaks they wore in cold weather.**

From Croy Hill, Dunbartonshire

From Bridgeness near the Antonine Wall

Agricola decided to deal with the tribes further north in the Highlands. He built a new fortress at Inchtuthill near Perth. Then he attacked with his legionaries and a strong force of troops on horseback. This stone carving shows a Roman horseman riding over a group of Celtic warriors.

**Find:**

- **the Roman soldier using a spear. What advantage would he have against foot soldiers?**
- **the helmet he is wearing. Centurions, officers in charge of a century of eighty soldiers, had plumes in their helmets.**
- **his cloak. Centurions had red cloaks which could be easily seen.**
- **the defeated Celtic warriors. How are they dressed? What has happened to them? Why would the Romans make this kind of carving?**

## The Battle of Mons Graupius

The Celtic tribes banded together to try to stop the Roman advance. The two armies met in battle at a place the Romans called Mons Graupius. No one is sure exactly where this was. The tribes were forced to give way and hide in the forests and mountains. They went on attacking smaller groups of Romans whenever they had the chance.

This is how a Roman writer called Tacitus, the son-in-law of Agricola, described later what happened at Mons Graupius.

The Roman discipline triumphed. While the enemy were in disorder the Roman troops kept their fighting order.

Agricola ordered his men to fight at close quarters. The enemy had only small shields and swords with no sharp point for thrusting.

The horsemen broke the ranks of the Caledonians and rode round to take them from behind. They left 10,000 dead on the field. Bodies, arms and cut off limbs lay all around. The Romans lost only 360.

Do you think a Celtic warrior would have described the battle in this way? We only know one side of the story because the Celts did not write.

After his victory Agricola thought he could conquer the rest of Scotland but a year later the Roman emperor ordered Agricola to go back to Rome. The Roman soldiers tried to destroy their forts before they left.

## The Roman walls

The tribes in the north attacked the settled places in the south whenever they could. Forty years after Agricola left, the Emperor Hadrian visited Britain. He ordered a huge stone wall built right across the country to keep out the wild people of the north. Hadrian's Wall took six years to build. There is a picture of it on page 40.

Later The Antonine Wall made of turfs on a stone base was built further north. It was more than 3 metres high. There were nineteen forts and look-out towers all along the wall. In front there was a deep ditch which was hard to cross. Only Roman soldiers were allowed in the space between the wall and the ditch. Behind the wall was a road where soldiers could move quickly. The map shows the two walls.

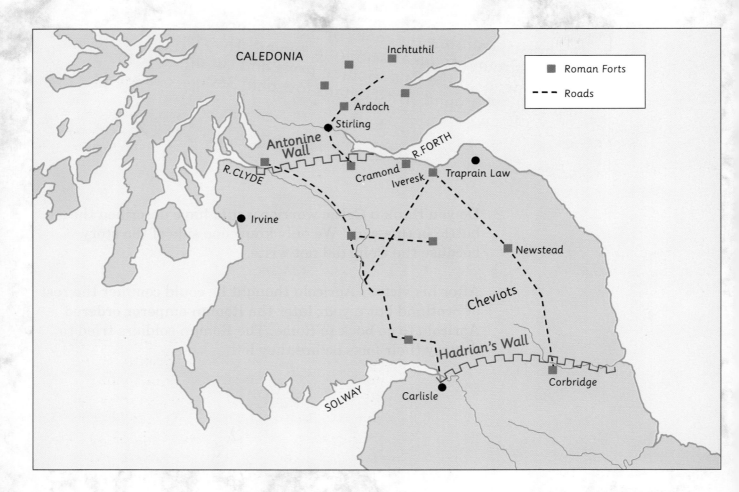

**Find the two rivers linked by The Antonine Wall. Why was this a good place to build it?**

The Romans often marked something important by putting up a carved monument or sculpture. When the soldiers of the Second Legion had built a long section of the Antonine Wall, they put up this carved stone slab to mark the distance.

From Bridgeness

An important person wearing a long toga is standing in front of an altar. He is making an offering of wine to the gods.

**Find:**

◆ the man wearing the toga.
◆ the altar.
◆ the bowl holding the wine.
◆ the pig, sheep and ox to be sacrificed.
◆ the man making music.
◆ the sign of the Second Legion being held up.

### Toga

**A long piece of cloth draped round the body. It was worn by Roman citizens.**

When the Romans at last left Britain after four hundred years, they had not had a great effect on Scotland. The tribes of the north had come together to fight them. Antonine's Wall held back the Celtic tribes for only forty years. The Romans left and went back south to Hadrian's Wall. Now and then they sent out patrols to Scotland. The Roman soldiers did not like to go into the forests and mountains of the north in small groups. Often the Caledonians attacked them. There was never peace as in the south of Britain.

## Hidden treasure

Nearly 2,000 Roman silver coins were found
buried in this jar near the Antonine Wall.

**Why do you think these coins were buried?**

Even today people are still finding things from Roman times.